Lennon & McCartney Piano Songs FOR DUMMIES®

Performance Notes by
Adam Perlmutter

ISBN: 978-1-4234-9605-2

HAL•LEONARD®
CORPORATION

7777 W. BLUEMOUND RD. P.O. BOX 13819 MILWAUKEE, WI 53213

Visit Hal Leonard Online at
www.halleonard.com

Table of Contents

Introduction

· ·

Welcome to *Lennon & McCartney Piano Songs For Dummies.* In this book, you'll find everything you need to play some of the greatest songs of The Beatles, from 1962's "Love Me Do" to 1969's "Across the Universe."

About This Book

For each song, I include a bit of background information to satisfy the historically curious. This information is followed by a variety of tidbits that struck me as I made my way through the teaching of these songs, including some of the following:

✔ A run-down of the parts you need to know.

✔ A breakdown of some of the chord progressions important to playing the song effectively.

✔ Some of the critical information you need to navigate the sheet music.

✔ Some tips and shortcuts you can use to expedite the learning process.

In many cases, you may already know how to do a lot of this. If so, feel free to skip over those familiar bits.

How to Use This Book

The music contains vocal and piano parts and guitar frames for each song. And included throughout are handy performance notes that help you learn how to play these songs and understand how they work. I recommend that you first play through the song, and then practice all the main sections and chords. From there, you can add the tricks and treats of each one — and there are many. Approach each song one section at a time and then assemble the sections together in a sequence. This technique helps to provide you with a greater understanding of how the song is structured, and enables you to play it through more quickly.

In order to follow the music and my performance notes, you need a basic understanding of scales and chords. But if you're not a wiz, don't worry. Just spend a little time with the nifty tome *Music Theory For Dummies* by Michael Pilhofer and Holly Day (Wiley), and with a little practice, you'll be on your way to entertaining family and friends.

Glossary

As you might expect, I use quite a few musical terms in this book. Some of these may be unfamiliar to you, so here are a few right off the bat that can help your understanding of basic playing principles:

- ✔ **Arpeggio:** Playing the notes of a chord one at a time rather than all together.

- ✔ **Bridge:** Part of the song that is different from the verse and the chorus, providing variety and connecting the other parts of the song to each other.

- ✔ **Coda:** The section at the end of a song, which is sometimes labeled with the word "coda."

- ✔ **Chorus:** The part of the song that is the same each time through, usually the most familiar section.

- ✔ **Hook:** A familiar, accessible, or sing-along melody, lick, or other section of the song.

- ✔ **Verse:** The part of the song that tells the story; each verse has different lyrics, and each song generally has between two and four of these.

Icons Used in This Book

In the margins of this book are several handy icons to help make following the performance notes easier:

A reason to stop and review advice that can prevent personal injury to your fingers, your brain, or your ego.

These are optional parts, or alternate approaches that those who'd like to find their way through the song with a distinctive flair can take. Often these are slightly more challenging routes, but encouraged nonetheless, because there's nothing like a good challenge!

This is where you will find notes about specific musical concepts that are relevant but confusing to non-musical types — stuff that you wouldn't bring up, say, at a frat party or at your kid's soccer game.

You get lots of these tips, because the more playing suggestions we can offer, the better you'll play. And isn't that what it's all about?

Across the Universe

Words and Music by John Lennon and Paul McCartney

The Ballad of John and Yoko

Words and Music by John Lennon and Paul McCartney

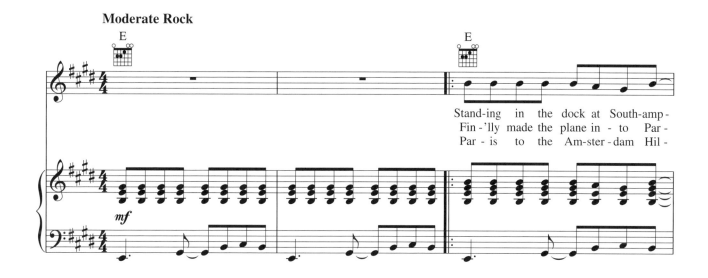

All My Loving

Words and Music by John Lennon and Paul McCartney

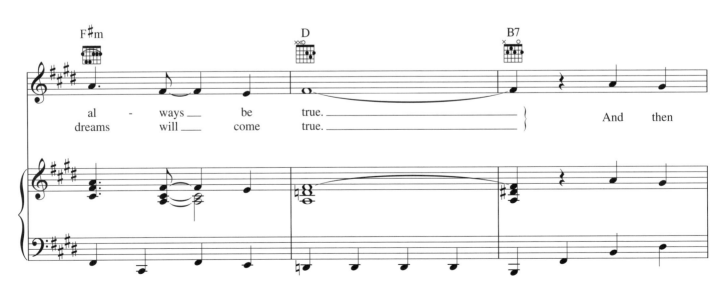

And I Love Her

Words and Music by John Lennon and Paul McCartney

Because

Words and Music by John Lennon and Paul McCartney

Don't Let Me Down

Words and Music by John Lennon and Paul McCartney

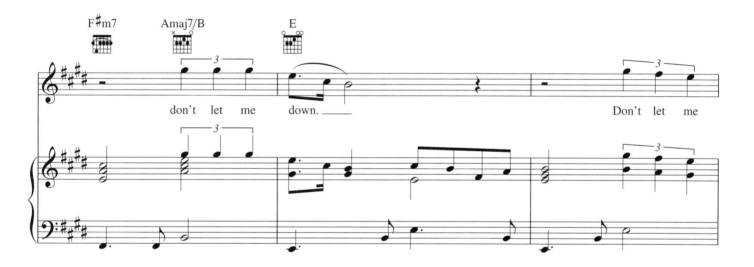

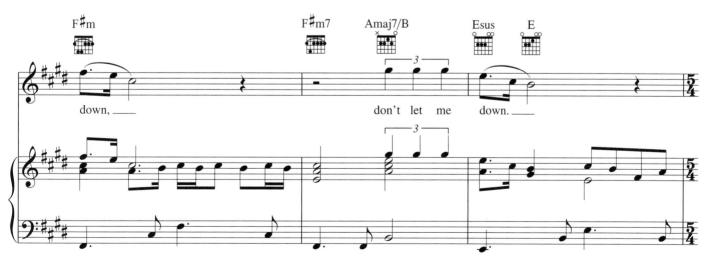

Can't Buy Me Love

Words and Music by John Lennon and Paul McCartney

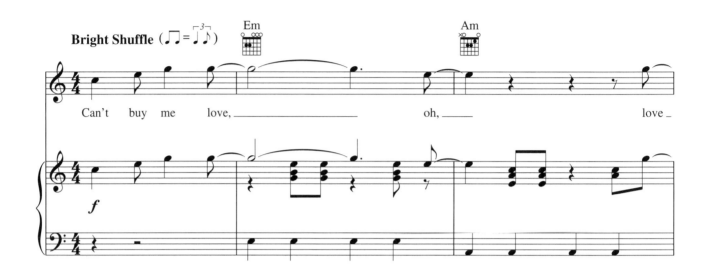

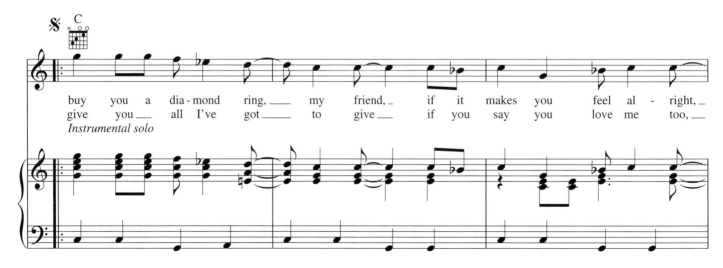

Drive My Car

Words and Music by John Lennon and Paul McCartney

The Fool on the Hill

Words and Music by John Lennon and Paul McCartney

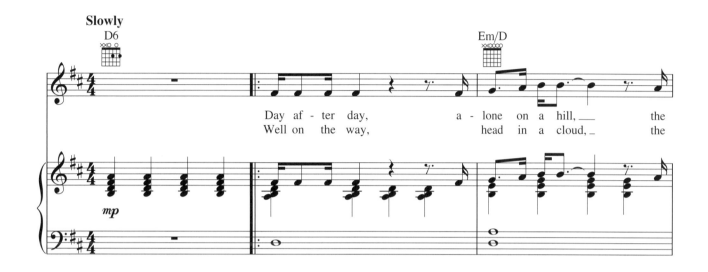

Day af - ter day, a - lone on a hill, ___ the
Well on the way, head in a cloud, ___ the

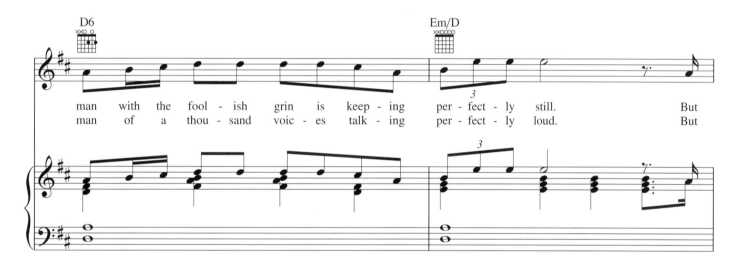

man with the fool - ish grin is keep - ing per - fect - ly still. But
man of a thou - sand voic - es talk - ing per - fect - ly loud. But

no - bod - y wants to know ___ him, they can see that he's just ___ a fool. ___ And
no - bod - y ev - er hears ___ him, or the sound he ap - pears ___ to make. ___ And

Eight Days a Week

Words and Music by John Lennon and Paul McCartney

not e - nough to show I care. ___

{ Ooh I need your

Love you ev - 'ry

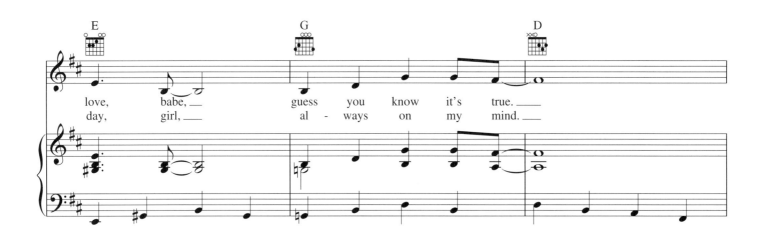

love, babe, ___ guess you know it's true. ___

day, girl, ___ al - ways on my mind. ___

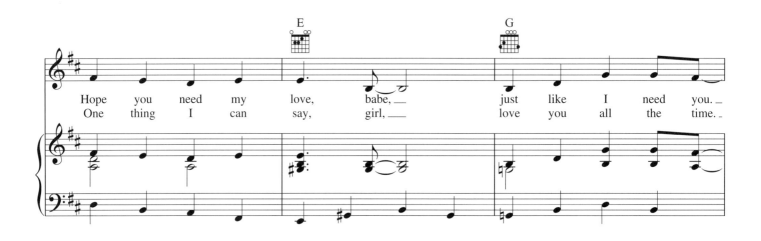

Hope you need my love, babe, ___ just like I need you.

One thing I can say, girl, ___ love you all the time. _

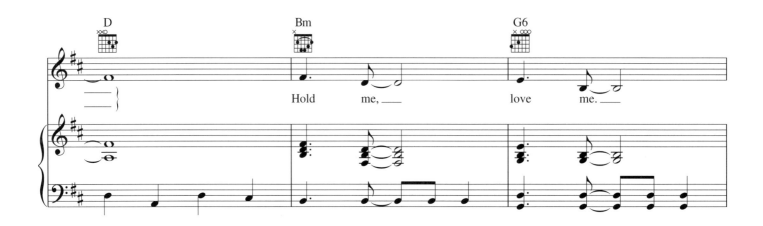

___ { Hold me, ___ love me. ___

From Me to You

Words and Music by John Lennon and Paul McCartney

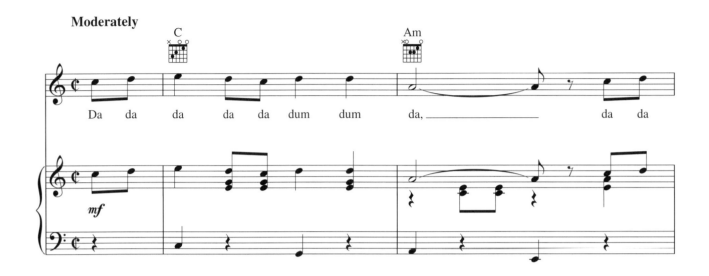

Da da da da da dum dum da, _____ da da

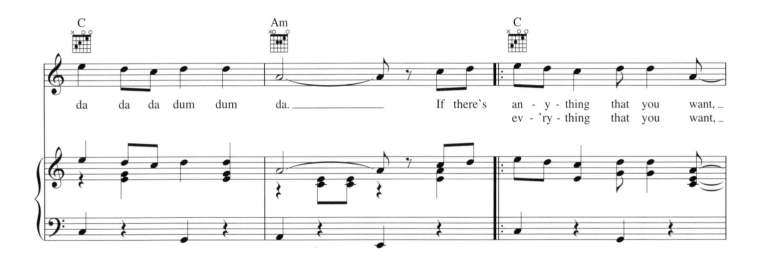

da da da dum dum da. _____ If there's an-y-thing that you want, _
ev-'ry-thing that you want, _

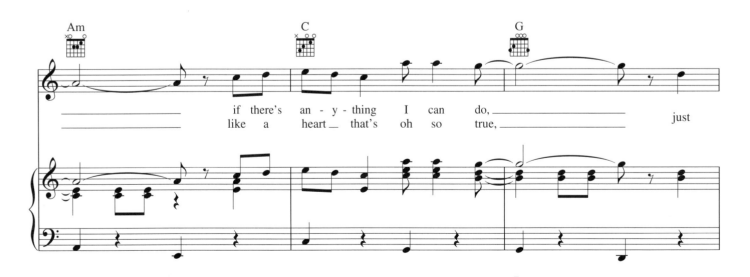

_____ if there's an-y-thing I can do, _____ just
_____ like a heart _ that's oh so true, _____

Golden Slumbers

Words and Music by John Lennon and Paul McCartney

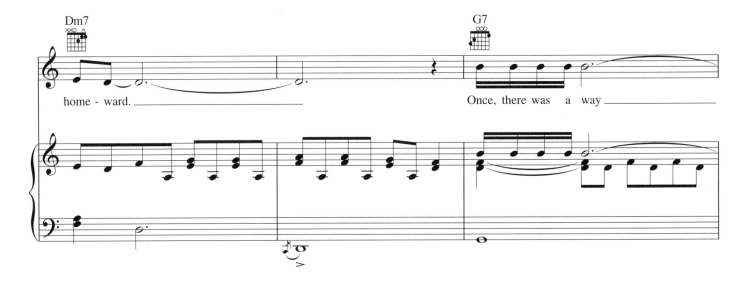

Good Day Sunshine

Words and Music by John Lennon and Paul McCartney

Good Night

Words and Music by John Lennon and Paul McCartney

I Will

Words and Music by John Lennon and Paul McCartney

Got to Get You into My Life

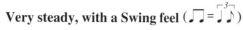

Words and Music by John Lennon and Paul McCartney

I was a - lone, __ I took a ride, ___ I did - n't know _ what I would find _
You did - n't run, _ you did - n't lie, ____ you knew I want - ed just to hold _
What can I do, __ what can I be? __ When I'm with you, __ I want to stay _

__ there. _
__ you. _
__ there. _

An - oth - er road __ where may - be I ___
And had you gone, _ you knew in time __
If I'm true __ I'll nev - er leave, __

could see an - oth - er kind of mind _____ there. _____
we'd meet a - gain, _____ for I had told _____ you. _____
and if I do, _____ I know the way _____ there. _____

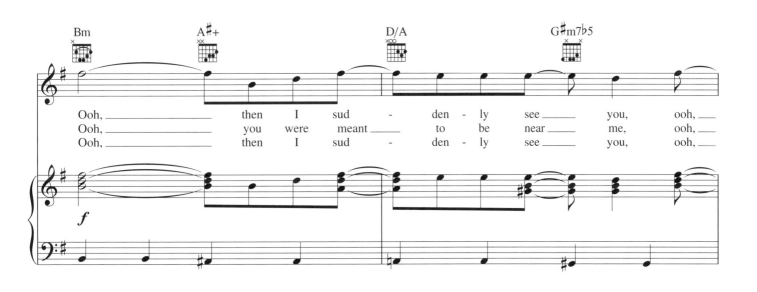

Ooh, _____ then I sud - den - ly see _____ you, ooh, _____
Ooh, _____ you were meant _____ to be near _____ me, ooh, _____
Ooh, _____ then I sud - den - ly see _____ you, ooh, _____

_____ did I tell _____ you I need _____ you ev - 'ry sin - gle
_____ and I want _____ you to hear _____ me say we'll be to -
_____ did I tell _____ you I need _____ you ev - 'ry sin - gle

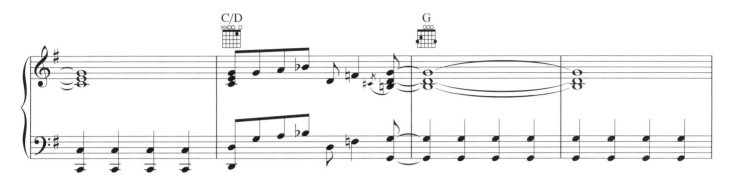

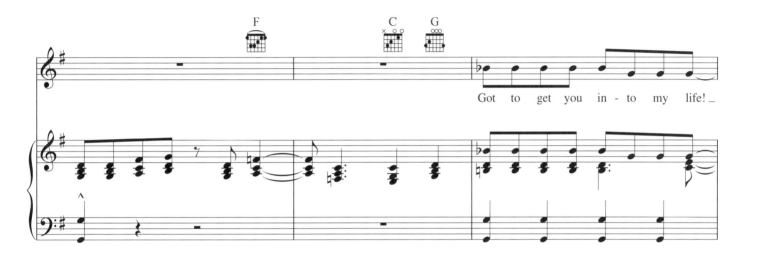

Got to get you in-to my life! _

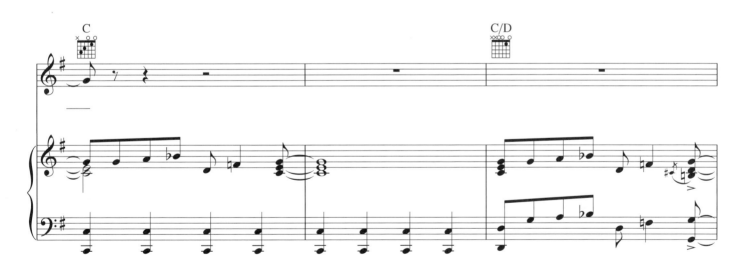

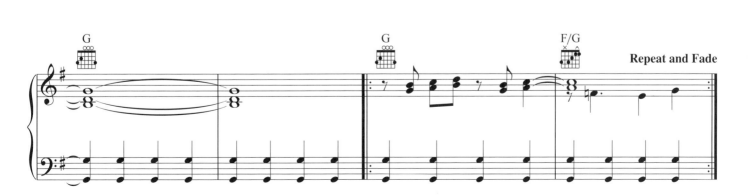

Repeat and Fade

Help!

Words and Music by John Lennon and Paul McCartney

Moderately, with a driving beat

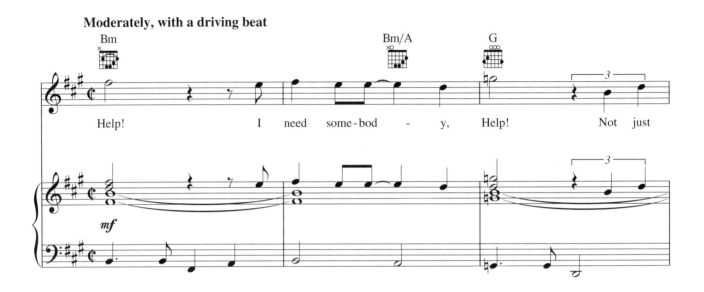

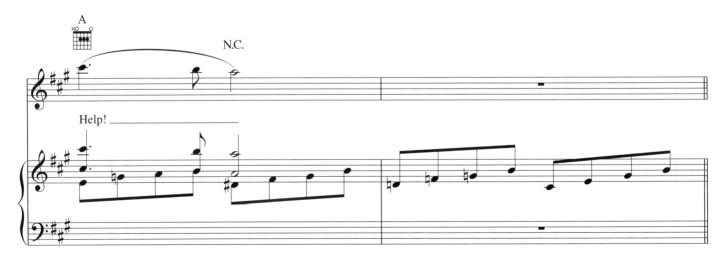

When I _____ was young - er, so _____ much young - er than _____ to - day, _____
And now _____ my life has changed _ in oh so man - y ways, _

_____
_____
I nev - er need - ed an - y - bod - y's
My in - de - pen - dence seems _ to

help in an - y way. _____ But now these
van - ish in the haze. _____ But ev - 'ry

days are gone, _____ I'm not so self - as - sured, _____
now and then _____ I feel so in - se - cure, _____

Hey Jude

Words and Music by John Lennon and Paul McCartney

I Am the Walrus

Words and Music by John Lennon and Paul McCartney

I Feel Fine

Words and Music by John Lennon and Paul McCartney

Bright Rock

I Saw Her Standing There

Words and Music by John Lennon and Paul McCartney

Bright Rock

Well, she was just ___ sev - en - teen, ___ and you
___ looked at me ___ and I,

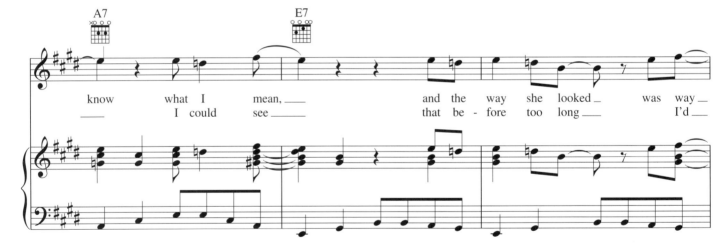

know what I mean, ___ and the way she looked _ was way _
___ I could see ___ that be - fore too long ___ I'd

___ be - yond com - pare. ___ So,
___ fall in love with her. ___

I Want to Hold Your Hand

Words and Music by John Lennon and Paul McCartney

Performance Notes

Across the Universe (page 6)

Purportedly, John Lennon wrote "Across the Universe" following an argument with his then-wife Cynthia, whose words he perceived as "flowing like an endless stream." The song first appeared on *No One's Gonna Change Our World,* a 1969 benefit album for the World Wildlife Fund. The following year a different version was recorded on The Beatles' final album, *Let It Be.* Although Lennon complained that the song was never recorded properly, it was well received and in fact, four decades after it was written, it earned the distinction as the first song to have been transmitted into outer space.

Be sure to play "Across the Universe" slowly and flowing. One thing to look out for throughout is the use of shifting meters. In bar 7, for instance, the music moves to 5/4 from 4/4, then back to 4/4 in bar 8 before going to 2/4 in bar 10. To successfully negotiate these changes, count "one, two, three, four" throughout. Add a beat in the 5/4 bar ("one, two, three, four, five") and count two beats in the 2/4 bar ("one, two"), taking care to maintain a steady pulse as you change meters.

All My Loving (page 16)

Although Paul McCartney normally composed music before lyrics, the words came first with "All My Loving," which he started writing while shaving. McCartney originally conceived of the song as a country western number, but The Beatles recorded it in 1963 in a more decidedly British pop setting. Although it wasn't initially released in the U.S. as a single, "All My Loving" was one of the songs that helped The Beatles gain immense popularity here when they played it on their famous *The Ed Sullivan Show* debut (February 9, 1964).

Written in the key of E major, "All My Loving" is played with a *swing feel* — a rhythm commonly seen in blues, jazz, and other soulful idioms. To achieve a swing feel, wherever you see a pair of eighth notes, play the first note longer than the second (at about a 2:1 ratio between the two notes). It's almost like you're playing a dotted eighth note followed by a 16th note. But be sure not to play these rhythms in a mechanical way. Strive for a loose and bouncing feel, and play along with the recording if you find that the swing feel eludes you.

And I Love Her (page 20)

Another early Beatles favorite, "And I Love Her" was written primarily by Paul McCartney. Notably, this ballad, recorded with just acoustic instruments, was the group's first "unplugged" recording. The song was introduced on the group's third album, *A Hard Day's Night* (1964), and has since been covered by a stylistically diverse range of artists, from jazz (Roland Kirk) to R&B (Smokey Robinson & The Miracles), and even reggae (Bob Marley & The Wailers).

"And I Love Her" kicks off here in the key of E major/C♯ minor. Heads up on the key change to D minor in the second bar of the coda. Be sure to avoid slowing down the tempo when you change keys. Note that the very last chord of the piece isn't the expected D minor, but D major. This device — ending a minor-key piece or section with a major chord is known as a *Picardy third* (or *Tierce de Picardie*). You may have heard Picardy thirds in the works of classical composers like J.S. Bach and others.

The Ballad of John and Yoko *(page 11)*

"The Ballad of John and Yoko" is about the dealings that John Lennon and his wife, Yoko Ono, had with international authorities in the late 1960s. Musically speaking, the song isn't a ballad but an up-tempo number, replete with a Spanish guitar part borrowed from "Lonesome Tears in My Eyes," a 1956 song by the early rocker Johnny Burnette. When "The Ballad of John and Yoko" was first released in the spring of 1969, it generated controversy due to the words "Christ" and "crucify," and was banned from U.S. airwaves. Now it is a classic rock radio staple.

"The Ballad of John and Yoko" is shown here in the original rock-friendly key of E major. The song has a funky melody due to the use of two blue notes, the flatted seventh, D♮, and the flatted third, G♮. These alterations make the music sound much hipper than it otherwise would. To hear for yourself, try singing and playing the notes D♯ and G♯ wherever you see the notes D and G, respectively. Also note that one of the song's chords, B7 (B-D♯-F♯-A), contains a blue note — the flatted seventh — A♮.

Because *(page 24)*

Written primarily by John Lennon, "Because" is a ballad that resulted from an interesting compositional process. Lennon was apparently listening to Yoko Ono playing Ludwig van Beethoven's *Moonlight Sonata* at the piano when it struck him to ask her to run through the music backwards. Lennon then built on this *retrograde* (backward) version to write "Because," released on 1969's *Abbey Road*. Another interesting thing: "Because" was the only Beatles song to feature nine-voice harmony throughout. John Lennon, Paul McCartney, and George Harrison sang three-part harmony and overdubbed themselves three times to create this lush vocal effect.

Written here in the somewhat dark key of C♯ minor, "Because" has some sophisticated harmony. Chords like D♯m7♭5 (D♯-F♯-A-C♯), A13 (A-C♯-E-G-B-D-F♯), and A9 (A-C♯-E-G-B) help create richer sounds than those available from basic major and minor chords. The song also contains a handful of accidentals, so be sure to take things very slowly when learning this song, scanning ahead for sharps, flats, and naturals. Listen closely to the rich sonorities of the chords.

Can't Buy Me Love *(page 30)*

Paul McCartney was the main writer of "Can't Buy Me Love," a song not about harlotry as many have suspected, but about the one thing that matters most in life. The song first appeared in 1964, on the A side of The Beatles' sixth British single, and has since been covered by everyone from jazz singer Ella Fitzgerald to country guitarist Chet Atkins to cartoon characters Bugs Bunny and Daffy Duck.

"Can't Buy Me Love" is shown here in the key of C major. The song kicks off with the chorus, a move that was unusual for a pop song in 1964 but has since become standard. The music is fairly straightforward, but for a convincing performance it's crucial to nail the rhythms. First of all, the song is played with a swing feel. (See the notes for "All My Loving" for an explanation of this feel.) Then, there's a bit of *syncopation* (the displacement of strong beats and the accenting of weak beats) throughout, so pay close attention to where each note falls in the bar. In the pickup bar, for instance, the first note C falls on beat 2, the first G on the "and" of 3, and the second G on the "and" of 4, all weak beats.

Don't Let Me Down (page 27)

One of The Beatles' greatest love songs is "Don't Let Me Down," which an anguished John Lennon wrote for his wife, Yoko Ono. The 1969 studio recording was among a handful of Beatles songs to feature an outside member, the pianist Billy Preston, allegedly enlisted to encourage the group, who were bickering at the time, to get along. Preston didn't save The Beatles — they disintegrated the following year — but he added a wonderfully soulful layer to this emotional song.

Shown here in the original key of E major, this arrangement of "Don't Let Me Down" is fairly straightforward. There are, though, a couple of rhythmic elements to look out for. In bar 2 and elsewhere is a *quarter-note triplet,* or three quarter notes in the space usually taken up by two, indicated with a bracketed 3. To feel this rhythm, you might try counting eighth note triplets on each beat: "trip-uh-let, trip-uh-let," and so on. In the span of two beats, a quarter note will then fall on the first "trip," the first "let," and the second "uh." If this rhythm is giving you trouble, count and practice it extremely slowly, using just one note, until you feel it naturally. Look out, too, for the time signature shifts between 4/4 and 5/4 that occur twice in this song.

Drive My Car (page 34)

When Paul McCartney presented this song to The Beatles, it was kind of a mess; the lyrics, invoking diamond rings, were rather clichéd. But John Lennon came up with an automotive analogy for the tune and then everything fell right into place. "Drive My Car" first appeared on the album *Rubber Soul* (1965, UK; 1966, U.S.) and with its beep-beep refrain established itself as one of The Beatles' most playful numbers.

Although "Drive My Car" has an ambiguous tonality — it can be thought of as being in either D major or G major — the song is written here in the key of G. "Drive My Car" owes its insistently driving feel to a syncopated bass line. To achieve this feel, you might first try isolating the bass part. If necessary, *subdivide:* count "One-ee-and-uh, two-ee-and-uh, three-ee-and-uh, four-ee-and-uh." In bar 3, for instance, left-hand notes fall on the following italicized syllables: "*One*-ee-and-uh, two-ee-*and*-uh, *three*-ee-*and*-uh, *four*-ee-*and*-uh." After you've got the bass line down, you should be able to get the rest of the piece together fairly easily.

Eight Days a Week (page 40)

Paul McCartney was the primary writer of "Eight Days a Week," a song about extreme devotion. The malaprop title is credited to either an overemployed chauffeur commenting on his work schedule or to Ringo Starr, who was known to coin a clever phrase. First heard on 1964's *Beatles for Sale,* "Eight Days a Week" was not highly regarded by The Beatles; in fact, the group never even performed it in concert. That, however, didn't stop the song from becoming one of their most popular numbers.

"Eight Days a Week," written here in the bright key of D major, is built from a handful of basic chords — D, E, G, Bm, and A. But modifications to a few select chords keep things harmonically interesting. For instance, the first chord, D (add9), a D triad (D-F♯-A) with an added 9th (E), has a particularly rich sound. The following two bars contain *slash chords,* in which the letter to the left represents the chord and the letter to the right stands for the lowest note to be played. Slash chords are used here to provide a *pedal tone.* In the first four bars, the note D (the pedal tone) remains constant while the chords above it change.

The Fool on the Hill (page 37)

From 1967's *Magical Mystery Tour,* "The Fool on the Hill" is a song about a man regarded as foolish but actually full of wisdom. The piece started off, as did many Beatles numbers, with Paul McCartney composing a chord progression on the piano, and ended up as this lovely version, with its overdubbed flute choir, heard on the album. Although the song was never a hit for The Beatles, a cover version by Sergio Mendes & Brasil '66 went all the way to #6 on the U.S. charts in 1968.

In the key of D major, "The Fool on the Hill" has a particularly wistful quality, thanks largely to the incorporation of a D6 chord, a D triad (D-F♯-A) with an added 6th (B). To hear what a substantial contribution that one note makes, try playing just a D chord wherever you see D6 in the music. The use of minor 7th chords, minor triads with added 7ths like Em7 (E-G-B-D) and Dm7 (D-F-A-C), reinforce the wistfulness. Try removing the 7ths (D and C, respectively) from these chords to see how much plainer the music would sound without them.

From Me to You (page 44)

In the early '60s The Beatles were touring with an American singer, Helen Shapiro, who was much more popular than they were. That all soon changed. As they were riding between gigs, John Lennon and Paul McCartney wrote what was to become The Beatles' first #1 hit in the UK, "From Me to You," the title of which was inspired by a music column called "From You to Us." The group played the song on their first *The Ed Sullivan Show* appearance, which helped fuel the era's Beatlemania.

"From Me to You," played here in the easy key of C major, is in *cut time,* as indicated at the beginning by the time signature (¢). Feel this meter by counting in half notes, two per bar, rather than quarter notes. Also, you'll want to pay close attention to the rhythm of the seemingly simple bass line. Be mindful of the rests that occur on beats 2 and 4; release the notes on beats 1 and 3 right after you've played them. It might help to think about the "oom-pah" sound of a marching band tuba when playing through the bass part.

Golden Slumbers (page 48)

One day in Liverpool Paul McCartney saw the sheet music for a Thomas Dekker poem, "Cradle Song," on his stepsister's piano. McCartney wanted to play the song, but unable to read music, he took the first four lines of the poem and created his own tune, which came to be known as "Golden Slumbers." The song appears as part of a medley on The Beatles' 1969 masterpiece, *Abbey Road.*

Take "Golden Slumbers," shown in the key of C, at a moderate tempo, and play as expressively as possible. Pay close attention to the *articulation* provided throughout. In bar 3, for instance, an *accent* (>) calls for you to play the indicated note forcefully. The small note that precedes it is a *grace note* — play the G quickly, connecting it smoothly to the A. If the grace notes prove too difficult to play, simply omit them. In the bass clef of bar 18 and elsewhere are *tenuto* marks (–), which call for you to add a little space between the indicated notes. Being mindful of these details will help you play with expression.

Good Day Sunshine (page 51)

Paul McCartney was the primary writer of the radiantly optimistic song "Good Day Sunshine," a song that was undoubtedly influenced by the Lovin' Spoonful's "Daydream," with its positive vibrations and old-time feel. "Good Day Sunshine," heard on 1966's *Revolver*, is among The Beatles' most infectious tunes — so snappy, in fact, that it was used as the official wakeup music on several Space Shuttle missions.

The bulk of "Good Day Sunshine" contains just four simple chords: B, F♯, E7, and A. Unlike those in many pop songs, the chords don't belong to a single key; rather they are neighbors in the *circle of fifths,* a graphic representation of the relationship between all 12 keys in music. Because of this, the music sounds a little shifty. After the four-bar intro, the chords B and F♯ make the music seem as if it's in the key of B major. But in bar 11, with the arrival of the A chord, the music feels like it's in A major. Then, in bar 19, the music seems to shift back to B major. Finally, in the last bar, a modulation up a half step, from E7 to F7, makes for a little more fun disorientation.

Good Night (page 54)

John Lennon originally wrote "Good Night" as a lullaby for his son Julian. This gentle song with its lush orchestration was sung by Ringo Starr and appeared as the last track on *The Beatles [White Album]* (1968). "Good Night" has since been covered by a range of artists, including The Carpenters, Manhattan Transfer, and Barbra Streisand, among others, and was fittingly used by the rock band Coldplay as a closing number on their 2005-2006 tour.

It should be fairly easy to play "Good Night," shown here in G major. Although not indicated in the music, this song would benefit from a bit of *rubato,* holding back and pushing forward within the tempo. After you've learned the piece as written, play it very gently and flowing, speeding up a little and slowing down where it feels natural. A couple more things to note: On the last system of the piece, the X noteheads simply mean that the notes don't have a definite pitch. And above the last chord the *fermatas* (⌢) call for you to hold the notes as long as you'd like.

Got to Get You into My Life (page 60)

"Got to Get You into My Life," a song not about a person but about a certain illicit plant, was written primarily by Paul McCartney. It was the first Beatles tune to make prominent use of a brass section, inspired by the horns heard on Stax, Motown, and other soul record labels of the 1960s. Although "Got to Get You into My Life" was included on the 1966 album *Revolver,* it was not released in the U.S. as a single until a decade later (six years after The Beatles split up), after which it quickly reached #7 on the charts.

Key to nailing "Got to Get You into My Life," presented here in the key of G major, will be steadily playing the swing feel. (For a full explanation, see the performance notes to "All My Loving.") The song has plenty of eighth-note triplets, three evenly spaced notes in one beat, as indicated by a three above or below the beam. To get a feel for these rhythms, try counting "trip-uh-let, trip-uh-let" when you play through the song, making sure to keep a steady beat while doing so.

Help! (page 64)

John Lennon was the primary songwriter of "Help!" the title song of the 1965 Beatles film and album. Purportedly, the song deals with Lennon feeling overwhelmed by the group's meteoric rise to success. The tune, which went to #1 on both the British and American charts in the summer of '65, only helped bring the group even greater acclaim. And now it ranks as one of the "500 Greatest Songs of All Time," according to *Rolling Stone* magazine.

"Help!" is shown here in the bright key of A major. This arrangement incorporates some of the guitar arpeggios heard prominently on the original recording. Beginning in bar 6, as indicated by the slanted line, the left hand travels to the treble clef to play a guitar-like figure. In bars 7 and 8, when you run through the eighth-note pattern, imagine you're playing the guitar, letting the notes ring together as if they're being played on different strings. Pretending you're a guitarist throughout the rest of the arrangement, which has an abundance of syncopated block chords, will help you achieve a properly driving beat.

Hey Jude (page 68)

"Hey Jude" is another song that was written with John Lennon's son Julian in mind. Paul McCartney composed the song and originally called it "Hey Jules," to help comfort the young boy as his parents were tangled in a divorce. At just over seven minutes, "Hey Jude" was the longest single in pop history at the time of its release in 1968, paving the way for such extended songs as Derek and the Dominos' "Layla." It also immediately became one of The Beatles' most popular songs, hitting #1 in 12 different countries and selling more than five million copies that same year.

The piano-driven "Hey Jude" is shown here in the original key of F major. The music has quite a bit of syncopation and multilayered parts, so if you find yourself having trouble playing it, simply break things down: First learn the bass part, which contains repeating single-note lines and will be easy to sight-read. Next, work on the right-hand parts, first the melody (up-stemmed notes), then the accompaniment (down-stemmed) before attempting both parts simultaneously. After you're comfortable with that, you'll be ready to play all of these parts together.

I Am the Walrus (page 72)

Composed primarily by John Lennon, "I Am the Walrus" is a trippy nonsensical song written in response to Lennon learning that The Beatles' works were being analyzed in an English class at his alma mater, Quarry Bank High School. Lennon found it amusing that his songs were being studied so seriously, so he wrote lyrics designed to confuse both teacher and student. "I Am the Walrus" appeared on 1967's *Magical Mystery Tour* (1967); with its bizarre lyrics and equally strange orchestration it is the prototypical psychedelic rock song.

"I Am the Walrus," shown here in the key of A major, has some interesting structural stuff going on. Whereas most pop songs use a mix of major and minor chords, the chords here are strictly major. Also, all seven letters of the musical alphabet (A, B, C, D, E, F, and G) are found in the progression. The *outro* (last four bars) is particularly cool: Although the chord progression descends neatly down in stepwise motion (A–G–F–E7), the melody, found in the top note of each right-hand chord, moves in *contrary motion* (A, B, C, D). The Beatles' use of such compositional techniques made their music so much more sophisticated than typical pop/rock fare.

I Feel Fine (page 78)

John Lennon was the primary composer of "I Feel Fine," a song that began life as a bluesy guitar riff. When The Beatles were in the studio recording the tune, Lennon leaned his guitar against an amplifier and a howling sound — feedback — emerged. Although such a noise would've previously been regarded as undesirable, it was used on the record to introduce the song, paving the way for guitarists like Jimi Hendrix, who deliberately harnessed feedback as part of his style. Released as a single in 1964, "I Feel Fine" was a smash hit in both the UK and the U.S.

Although "I Feel Fine" is in the key of G major, it is presented in C due to the fact that many times F is played as F♮, for a bluesy sound. The song is very straightforward, but the melody has some *chromatic* notes, notes outside the key that might throw you off if you're trying to sing it. For example, on beat 4 of bar 10 there's a *chromatic passing tone* (a note that connects two pitches that are a step apart within a key), which bridges the C on beat 3 to D on the downbeat of the following bar. If you have trouble singing this note, use the piano as a reference and repeatedly sing the passage until you can do so without assistance.

I Saw Her Standing There (page 82)

Paul McCartney has told interviewers that early on in his musical education he took a cross-town bus just to find someone to show him how to play a 7th chord. This type of chord makes frequent appearances in "I Saw Her Standing There," which McCartney and Lennon wrote together using a bass riff borrowed from Chuck Berry. Always a crowd pleaser at Beatles concerts, this energetic song was a logical choice for the opening track of The Beatles 1963 debut album, *Please Please Me*. It remains one of the most significant rock songs ever written.

"I Saw Her Standing There" is played here in the rock-friendly key of E major. In that key, only the V chord (built on the fifth note B of the scale) is a 7th chord (B-D♯-F♯-A). But The Beatles also play the I and IV chords (respectively, E and A) as 7ths (E-G♯-B-D and A-C♯-E-G). In other words, they add flat 7ths (D and G) to the E and A chords. This makes everything sound a great deal more soulful, and more rocking. To hear the difference for yourself, try playing the song with regular E and A chords instead of the 7ths throughout.

I Want to Hold Your Hand (page 88)

In the early 1960s Beatles manager Brian Epstein was troubled by the group's lack of commercial success stateside, so he instructed John Lennon and Paul McCartney to write a song geared specifically toward the U.S. market. This resulted in "I Want to Hold Your Hand," released in late 1963, a charmingly innocent number that was the group's first #1 hit in the U.S. the following year. Although initially dismissed by some critics as a faddish song, "I Want to Hold Your Hand" continues to enthrall new generations of fans almost five decades after its release.

Shown here in G major, "I Want to Hold Your Hand" has a structure more similar to those standards in the Great American Songbook (works by Irving Berlin, George & Ira Gershwin, Cole Porter, and so on) than the average rock song. A typical standard has a 32-bar AABA form, in which each section is 8 bars long. The A sections have the same music, and the B section (or bridge) has contrasting material. "I Want to Hold Your Hand" has a modified AABAA version of this form.

I Will *(page 57)*

In the late 1960s, The Beatles took a trip to Rishikesh, India, to study with Maharishi Mahesh Yogi. The group also worked on a handful of songs while in India, including "I Will," a love song for Paul McCartney's future wife, Linda Eastman. The tune, which appears on the double-disc *The Beatles [White Album]* (1968), has a stark instrumentation; just voice, guitar, and percussion help emphasize its earnest message, one of uncommon devotion.

"I Will" is arranged here in the original key, F major. One element that makes the studio version so warm is that instead of playing the bass line on his famous violin bass, McCartney sang it. For fun, you might try recreating that effect with a male voice singing the down-stemmed notes of the piano accompaniment in the bass clef. Have another singer tackle the vocal melody and a third vocalist add the harmony notes, shown throughout as cue-size noteheads in the top staves of each system beginning in bar 11. At the same time, strum along gently on a guitar using the chord frames shown above the vocal staff, and maybe even add percussion using whatever instruments or objects you happen to have handy.

I'll Follow the Sun *(page 106)*

Paul McCartney wrote "I'll Follow the Sun," from the point of view of an underappreciated lover, when he was a teenager. Around 1960 The Beatles recorded a rough version of the song in a rock 'n' roll setting. But most people are familiar with the official 1964 version (from the album *Beatles for Sale*) of the song, with its uncanny blend of folk instrumentation and pop sophistication, a somewhat underappreciated gem in The Beatles' catalog.

"I'll Follow the Sun," shown here in C major, is a guitar-driven song, so it might be fun to dust off that old six-string for this number. First get acquainted with the chord frames shown above the vocal staff. Then try *arpeggiating* the chords. Play the chord as shown, and pick selected individual notes in a pattern similar to the one seen in the eighth notes of the first two bars of the piano part. Let the individual notes ring together throughout.

If I Fell *(page 112)*

Perhaps addressing the ambivalence he felt in his first marriage, John Lennon was the primary writer of the earnest ballad "If I Fell." The song first appeared on the 1964 Beatles album *A Hard Day's Night.* While on tour that same year, Lennon and McCartney were known to goof around on "If I Fell," sometimes introducing it as "If I Fell Over" and noticeably suppressing their laughter while singing it. Still, it caught on as one of the greatest of all rock 'n' roll love songs.

"If I Fell," written here in the key of D major, demonstrates Lennon and McCartney's formal and harmonic sophistication. Atypical for a pop song, it has an introduction (bars 1-8) that isn't repeated anywhere else in the song. Not only that, the introduction is in Db major, a half step below the song's main key. The verse is built from a D-Em-F#m-Fdim progression that would be at home in a George Gershwin or Cole Porter tune.

Julia *(page 116)*

When The Beatles traveled to Rishikesh, India in 1968, they did a fair amount of meditating. In the process, John Lennon found himself reflecting on his feelings about his mother, "Julia," who was hit by a car and killed when he was a teenager. During this time the singer-songwriter Donovan was travelling with The Beatles, and he taught Lennon how to play guitar in the fingerstyle manner. So, using his newfound guitar skills Lennon wrote "Julia" with his mother in mind. The song is heard on The Beatles' 1968 *White Album* and is one of the most intimate tunes Lennon ever recorded, featuring just him and guitar alone.

In the D-major piano arrangement of "Julia" shown here, the music is straightforward and should not present any technical problems. Because the song is guitar-based, you might try playing it on a six-string using a fingerstyle technique. As you did for "I'll Follow the Sun," first learn the chords. Then try fingerpicking some arpeggios.

Love Me Do *(page 122)*

John Lennon and Paul McCartney wrote one of The Beatles' earliest songs, "Love Me Do," in 1958 when they were skipping school. Several years later, when The Beatles were recording the song with producer George Martin, he tinkered around with it a bit, having John play harmonica and, to Ringo Starr's chagrin, calling in a session drummer to re-record the song. Initially, employees at The Beatles' record label Parlophone were dubious of "Love Me Do." But when the song was released as The Beatles' first single in 1962, it crept its way to #17 in the UK, and two years later hit #1 on the U.S. charts.

When you play "Love Me Do," shown here in G major, be sure to really swing those eighth notes for the proper rhythmic feel. And check out the cleverly simple form of the song. The whole tune is built on just three basic chords: G7, C, and D. The intro (bars 1-8), verses (9-21 and 32-44), and outro (45-46) feature just two of the chords, C and G7, and the middle eight or *bridge* (24-31) incorporates all three. Despite this rudimentary setting, The Beatles still sound downright original.

Lucy in the Sky with Diamonds *(page 126)*

Many have assumed that "Lucy in the Sky with Diamonds" (from *Sgt. Pepper's Lonely Hearts Club Band,* 1967) is a song about drugs, because its acronym is identical to that of a certain hallucinogen. But in fact, the Lucy who inspired the song was a classmate of Lennon's son Julian. The younger Lennon painted a picture of Lucy with a starry-skied background and gave his artwork the title that found its way into a Beatles song. And the imagery contained in that song comes not from an acid trip but from a more innocent source — Lewis Carroll's *Alice in Wonderland.*

"Lucy in the Sky" kicks off here in the key of A major and in waltz time, that is, three quarter notes per bar. Be sure to watch out for the song's shifts in key and meter. When playing the music, scan ahead so that you'll be prepared for these changes. In the pre-chorus, starting in bar 24, heads up on the key change to B♭ major. At the chorus (bar 36), the music changes key, to D major, and meter, to 4/4 time. Note that the dotted half note of the previous 3/4 bar is equal to a half note in the 4/4 bar. In other words, a full bar of 3/4 is now equivalent to a half bar of 4/4.

Ob-La-Di, Ob-La-Da (page 130)

Paul McCartney was the primary writer of "Ob-La-Di, Ob-La-Da." At the time the song was written, in the late 1960s, reggae and highlife music were enjoying popularity in Britain, and McCartney borrowed the title from a reggae outfit called Jimmy Scott and His Obla Di Obla Da Band. Although McCartney's bandmates supposedly disliked "Ob-La-Di, Ob-La-Da," it proved one of the most popular songs on *The Beatles [White Album]* (1968) and further, it helped stir the reggae craze of that era.

"Ob-La-Di, Ob-La-Da," presented here in the key of B♭ major, is a rather simple song with straightforward chords and not a single *accidental* (added sharp, flat, or natural) to be found in the piece. To perform it properly, you'll want to concentrate on the rhythm. Start with the bass line on its own and strive for a loose, limping feel like that heard on a typical reggae song. Be sure to release the sound wherever you see a rest. Then, before combining parts, work on the right-hand accompaniment, found in the down-stemmed notes of the treble clef, where you'll often add a chord on beats 2 and 4, observing the rests on beats 1 and 3.

Oh! Darling (page 136)

When Paul McCartney began recording his song "Oh! Darling," he found his voice to be too clear. He wanted to sound a little rough, as if he'd been performing the song in a club for weeks. After a few days of singing the song, McCartney finally achieved the tone he had in mind and the finished recording — a down-and-dirty number indebted to classic New Orleans R&B — was released on The Beatles' *Abbey Road* (1969).

Shown here in the key of A major, "Oh! Darling" is in 12/8, a time signature containing 12 eighth notes per bar and associated with R&B and other soulful idioms. When learning the song, count slowly and carefully. Put a little emphasis on each downbeat, like this: "*One,* two, three; *two,* two, three; *three,* two, three; *four,* two, three." Another thing to note: The song starts with an *augmented* (E+) chord, which can be thought of as an E triad (E-G♯-B) with a raised fifth (B♯). Note the way in which this tense chord commands the listener's attention before it resolves to the A major chord in the first full bar.

Paperback Writer (page 140)

Paul McCartney wrote "Paperback Writer" about an author of questionable merit, after helping some friends open the Indica Bookshop in London in the mid 1960s. Released as a single in 1966, "Paperback Writer" was built from an ultra-heavy bass line and mixed loud, for a sound that was a bit edgier than previous Beatles efforts. And as the first #1 Beatles hit not about love, the song was a bridge to the group's soon-to-come experiments with songwriting and arranging.

Although "Paperback Writer" is written here in the key of G major, it has more of a *modal* sound, specifically G *Mixolydian* (G–A–B–C–D–E–F), due to the frequent appearance of the note F♮. This gives the music a distinctly bluesy sound that is reinforced by the use of a blue note, the flat 3 (B♭), in the bass line. Speaking of the bass line, when you run through this part, play it forcefully rocking, with a distorted instrument in mind, because that was such a prominent part of the original recording.

Please Please Me (page 109)

A big fan of Roy Orbison, John Lennon wrote "Please Please Me" as a ballad in Orbison's somewhat emotional style. But producer George Martin found that version insipid, and suggested that The Beatles speed up the song. They did just that on the 1962 recording, which became their second UK single and first #1 on the British charts. After being released a couple of times in the U.S., the song finally peaked at #3 on the charts in March of 1964, shortly after The Beatles first appeared on *The Ed Sullivan Show.*

Taken at a moderate but rocking tempo, "Please Please Me" is shown here in the key of E major. Although the music should be fairly easy to play there are a number of chromatic notes in the vocal line that might trip you up. In the second bar of the second ending, for instance, you'll find what's known as a *chromatic lower neighbor* — the note B♯ (another spelling of the note C) below the C♯s that surround it. The same move appears transposed up a whole step (D♯ – D♮ – D♯) in the following bar. If you find yourself having trouble singing these notes, isolate those passages and use the piano as reference until you can sing everything with accuracy.

P.S. I Love You (page 144)

Paul McCartney wrote "P.S. I Love You" in 1962, when The Beatles were the house band at the Star Club in Hamburg, Germany. That same year, when the group recorded "P.S. I Love You" for Parlophone, they hoped to release the song as their first single. However, the singer Peggy Lee had a record with the same name, so "P.S. I Love You" first appeared in 1962 as the B side of "Love Me Do."

"P.S. I Love You," was one of The Beatles' earliest songs, but it has some pretty sophisticated chord work. In bar 5 and elsewhere is a chord not found in the key of D — C♯7, which would ordinarily resolve to an F♯ chord. But the C♯7 works nicely in this foreign context, providing a bit of a surprise while leading smoothly enough to the following D chord. Elsewhere in the song, B♭ and C7 chords are "borrowed" from the song's parallel key, D minor, lending a fleetingly ambiguous quality to the proceedings.

She Loves You (page 148)

Paul McCartney and John Lennon wrote "She Loves You" after playing a show in England with Roy Orbison and Gerry & The Pacemakers. The song started off as a call-and-response idea in which one of The Beatles would sing "She loves you" and the others would respond, "Yeah, yeah, yeah." "She Loves You" was released as a single in both the U.S. and the UK in 1963. Although the lyric "Yeah, yeah, yeah" is totally innocuous by today's standards, in the early 1960s UK it was a scandalous abuse of the English language.

Like many Beatles songs, "She Loves You," written here in the key of G major, has some interesting and subtle details that reveal the group's wide range of musical influences. The song ends, for example, on guitarist George Harrison's G6 chord — a G triad (G-B-D) with an added 6th (E). Supposedly, The Beatles producer George Martin questioned the use of this chord, more at home in swing and big band music than in rock 'n' roll. But The Beatles prevailed, and this seemingly incongruous chord made for a great rock coda.

She's Leaving Home *(page 153)*

After reading a newspaper story about a young girl who ran away from home, John Lennon and Paul McCartney were inspired to write one of their most poignant songs, "She's Leaving Home." First heard on *Sgt. Pepper's Lonely Hearts Club Band* (1967), the song was one of several numbers on which The Beatles didn't play any instruments, but only sang. On the recording, Lennon and McCartney were accompanied by string players, as well as the harpist Sheila Bromberg, the first woman to play on a Beatles album.

"She's Leaving Home" is written here in the key of E major and like many Beatles songs it has a number of interesting things going on harmonically. In bar 5, the Bm chord (B-D-F♯) is borrowed from the parallel key of E minor. Note the use in bar 11 of a *secondary dominant* chord, F♯7, which is the *dominant* (chord built on the fifth note of the scale) of the original V chord (B7). Beginning in bar 13, there is an example of some *static* harmony; the music sits on that V chord (the basic harmony is B7) through bar 20, creating tension before resolving to the E chord in the following bar. All of these harmonic moves add richness to the song.

Strawberry Fields Forever *(page 158)*

Strawberry Fields was a Salvation Army home around the corner from John Lennon's childhood house in the Liverpool suburb of Woolton. That home later inspired the great Beatles song "Strawberry Fields Forever." Although the tune has some surreal lyrics, it, along with "Penny Lane," has a strong theme of nostalgia for Liverpool. When "Strawberry Fields" was released as a single in February 1967, many critics considered it The Beatles' best work to date. A great number of musicians also shared this view and were particularly influenced by the song's psychedelic overtones.

Shown here in the key of A major, "Strawberry Fields Forever" is filled with shifting meters, between 4/4, 3/4, and 2/4. So when you're learning the song, take things very slowly at first, constantly looking for upcoming time signature changes. When changing between meters, if you're not focused you might find yourself slowing down momentarily, so strive to move seamlessly between meters. Count carefully, and if necessary, use a metronome so that you don't stray from the basic pulse.

Ticket to Ride *(page 162)*

The inspiration for the title "Ticket to Ride" is unclear. Paul McCartney said it made reference to a British Railway ticket, whereas John Lennon claimed it described the clean-bill-of-health cards carried by street workers in Hamburg, Germany. What is clear is that this 1965 single, with its heavy guitars and bombastic drumming, signaled a change not just in The Beatles' direction but in that of rock in general.

A performance of "Ticket to Ride," shown here in A major, benefits from rhythmic precision, so you'll want to take things slowly and count carefully when learning the song. In the intro (first four bars) there are some quarter-note triplets. See the performance notes to "Don't Let Me Down" for an explanation of how to feel this rhythm. Subdivide in the verse, if needed.

We Can Work It Out (page 166)

"We Can Work It Out" is a song that reveals the different personalities of John Lennon and Paul McCartney. The latter's contribution, the verses, show McCartney's sunny optimism, whereas the bridge ("Life is very short, and there's no time…") emphasizes Lennon's more pessimistic outlook. It has been inferred that McCartney wrote his part of "We Can Work It Out" for his then girlfriend, the English actress Jane Asher. Although things actually didn't work out for them, the song was a #1 hit for The Beatles on both sides of the Atlantic.

"We Can Work It Out," arranged here in D major, cleverly uses harmony to support the emotional feel of each section. McCartney's bright verses are filled with sunny major chords: D, C, G, A. In contrast, Lennon's darker bridge centers around a Bm chord with a descending bass line (Bm–Bm/A–Bm/G).

When I'm Sixty-Four (page 172)

Paul McCartney wrote the charmingly infectious "When I'm Sixty-Four" when he was all of 16 years old. Although the song first appeared on 1967's masterpiece *Sgt. Pepper's Lonely Hearts Club Band,* The Beatles had been playing it in concert for years whenever their amplifiers overheated. And although many in The Beatles' generation weren't big on "When I'm Sixty-Four" when it first came out, it now ranks among The Beatles most popular tunes.

It's possible to play this C-major arrangement of "When I'm Sixty-Four" exactly as written and sound pretty unexpressive. So, before tackling the song you should check out the original version, which has a clarinet trio playing an infectiously swinging accompaniment. When you run through the piano arrangement, try to capture the phrasing you heard on the original, paying close attention to where notes in both the singing and accompaniment are accented and where the rests occur.

With a Little Help from My Friends (page 178)

When John Lennon and Paul McCartney wrote "With a Little Help from My Friends" they originally called it "Bad Finger Boogie," because Lennon had injured his index finger and was forced to use his middle finger when composing the melody at the piano. The song first appeared on *Sgt. Pepper's Lonely Hearts Club Band* (1967), sung by the imaginary leader of that fictitious band, Billy Shears. It has been covered extensively, most famously by Joe Cocker, in 1968.

Played here in E major, "With a Little Help from My Friends" makes extensive use of a technique known as *call and response.* A leader, in this case Billy Shears (drummer Ringo Starr) sings a line, while others (the rest of the band) reply. In the music, the lyrics of the responses are all shown in parentheses. Another thing to note: With the exception of the final note of the song, the call phrases span only the interval of a perfect 5th, the E above middle C to B. That's because the melody was composed with Starr, who had a limited vocal range, in mind.

Yesterday (page 169)

One night around 1965, Paul McCartney dreamt the music for a melancholic ballad and woke up to write it down. Worried that he had subconsciously plagiarized the song, temporarily titled "Scrambled Eggs," McCartney waited until he confirmed that the music was indeed original before he wrote the lyrics to what would become "Yesterday." With more than 3,000 recorded versions, "Yesterday" is the world's most covered song.

"Yesterday" begins in the key of F major, but sometimes ventures into the relative key of D minor. For instance, the song starts off clearly in F, on an F major chord, but by bar 5, with the arrival of a D minor chord, seems to be in the key of D minor. When the verse ends in bar 9 on an F chord, by the second bar of the bridge (bar 11), the D minor chord feels sort of like home again. This tonal ambiguousness helps underscore the brooding nature of the lyrics.

You Won't See Me (page 186)

"You Won't See Me" is another song that Paul McCartney wrote in response to his relationship with Jane Asher, but unlike "We Can Work It Out," this one isn't quite so optimistic. The Motown-inspired "You Won't See Me" appeared on 1965's *Rubber Soul*. Notably, it is one of the few songs where McCartney sings lower harmony while John Lennon and George Harrison sing the higher lines.

In composing "You Won't See Me," shown here in A major, Paul McCartney started with a simple chromatic move, the descending line E-D#-D♮-C#. (On the original recording the background vocals sing this line starting on the second verse.) This chromatic line suggested the chord progression A-B7-D-A, played twice in bars 1-8 of the verse. In the ninth bar of the verse, the line is transposed up a minor 3rd to G-F#-F♮-E, yielding the progression A7-D-Dm-A. To hear for yourself how these chromatic lines work in context, try singing them as you play the piano.

You've Got to Hide Your Love Away (page 182)

John Lennon had the music of Bob Dylan in mind when he wrote "You've Got to Hide Your Love Away," a folk-inspired acoustic song with scratchy singing and spare accompaniment. "You've Got to Hide Your Love Away" was a highlight of The Beatles' album *Help!* (1965) and has been covered extensively throughout the years, most notably by The Beach Boys, Elvis Costello, and Pearl Jam.

"You've Got to Hide Your Love Away" is arranged here in the key of G major and in 6/8 time, which means there are six eighth notes per bar. Ultimately, you'll want to feel this meter in two, which you can do by tapping on the first and fourth eighth notes of each bar. But to get the hang of the meter, you might start by tapping all six beats in a bar counting: "*One*-two-three, *four*-five-six," emphasizing the first and fourth beats. Pay close attention to the placement of each note. In the first bar, for instance, two 16th notes are played on beats 2, 3, 5, and 6.

I'll Follow the Sun

Words and Music by John Lennon and Paul McCartney

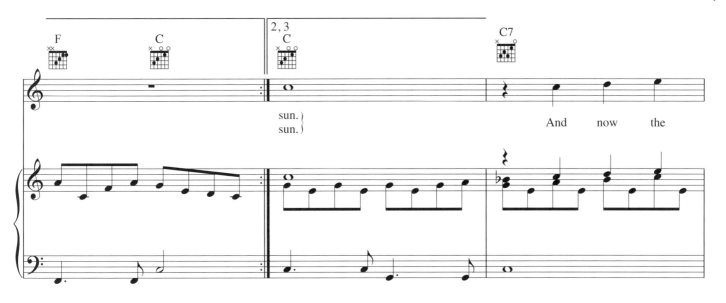

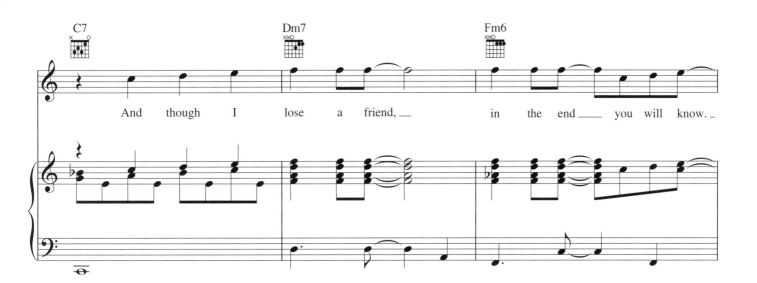

Please Please Me

Words and Music by John Lennon and Paul McCartney

Moderately with a beat

If I Fell

Words and Music by John Lennon and Paul McCartney

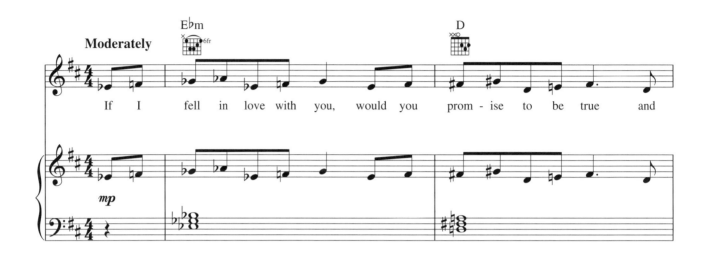

If I fell in love with you, would you prom-ise to be true and

help me un-der-stand? 'Cause I've been in love be-fore, and I

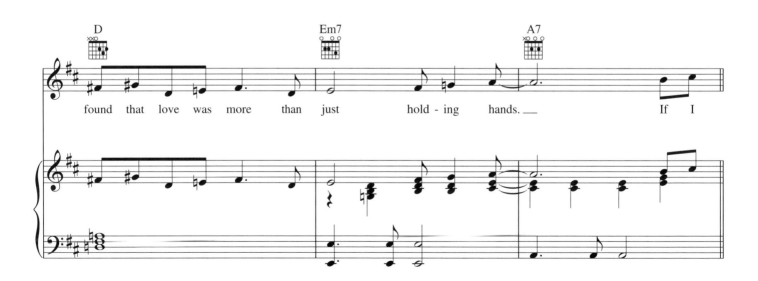

found that love was more than just hold-ing hands. If I

cry   when she learns we are two. ____   'Cause I

she learns we are two. ____   If I fell in love with

you.

Julia

Words and Music by John Lennon and Paul McCartney

Moderately slow and wistfully

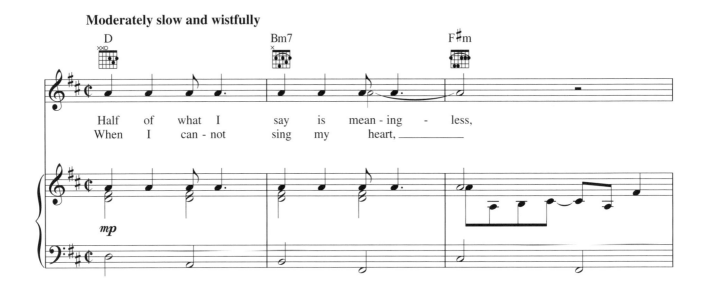

Half of what I say is mean-ing-less,

When I can-not say sing my heart, _____

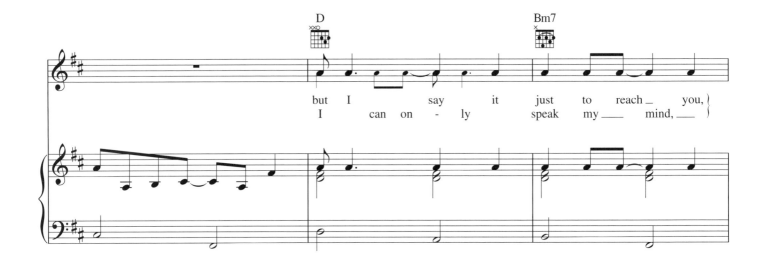

but I say it just to reach ___ you,

I can on-ly speak my ___ mind, ___

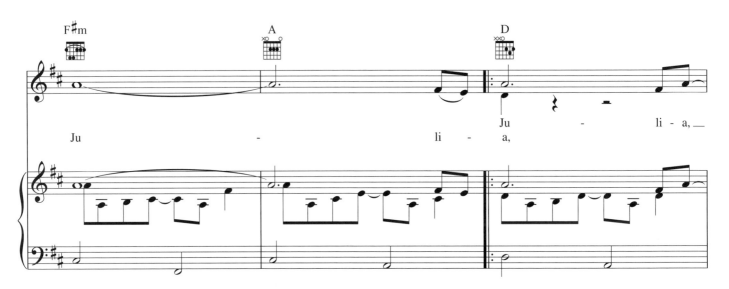

Ju - li - a,

Ju - li - a,

Love Me Do

Words and Music by John Lennon and Paul McCartney

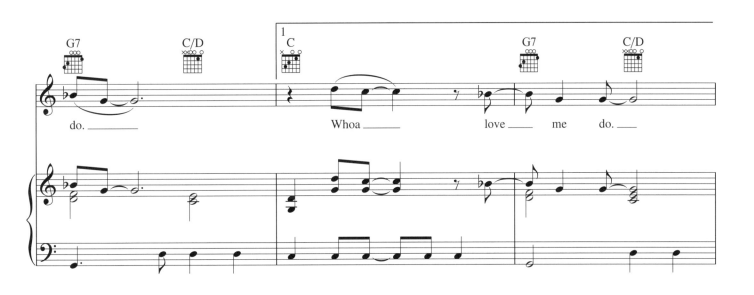

Lucy in the Sky with Diamonds

Words and Music by John Lennon and Paul McCartney

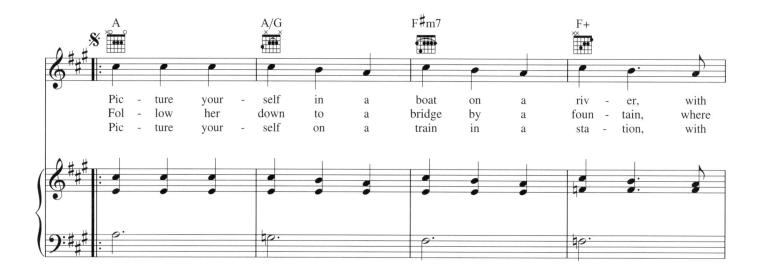

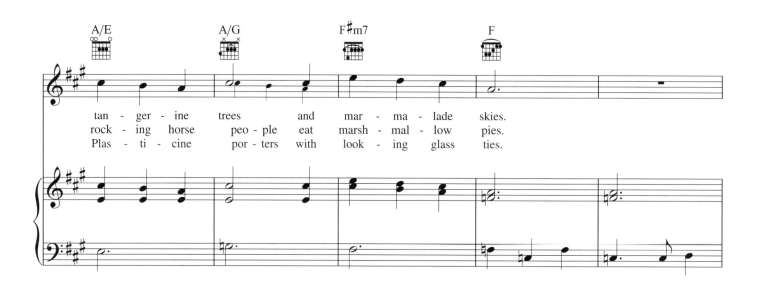

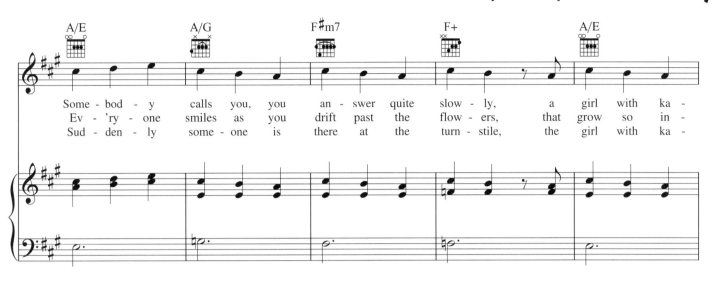

Some - bod - y calls you, you an - swer quite slow - ly, a girl with ka -
Ev - 'ry - one smiles as you drift past the flow - ers, that grow so in -
Sud - den - ly some - one is there at the turn - stile, the girl with ka -

lei - do - scope eyes.
cred - i - bly high.
lei - do - scope

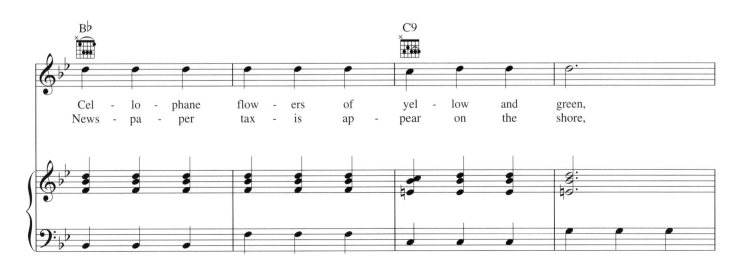

Cel - lo - phane flow - ers of yel - low and green,
News - pa - per tax - is ap - pear on the shore,

Ob-La-Di, Ob-La-Da

Words and Music by John Lennon and Paul McCartney

Oh! Darling

Words and Music by John Lennon and Paul McCartney

Paperback Writer

Words and Music by John Lennon and Paul McCartney

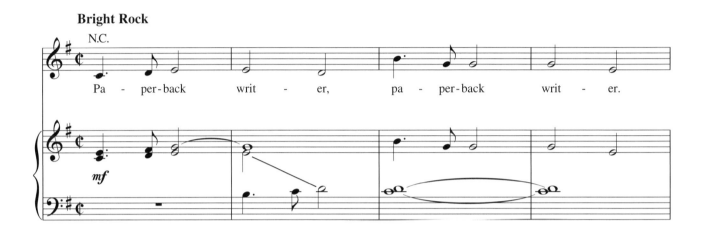

P.S. I Love You

Words and Music by John Lennon and Paul McCartney

Moderate Rock

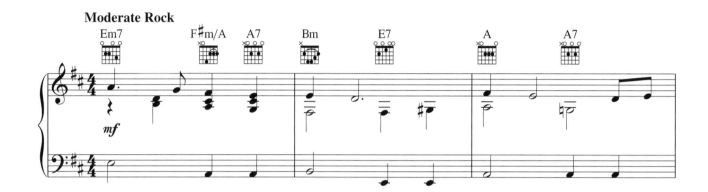

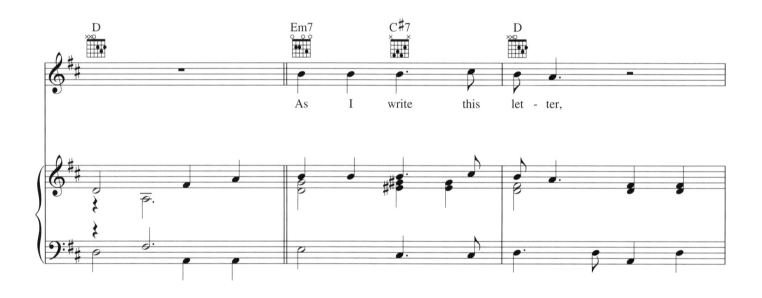

As I write this let - ter,

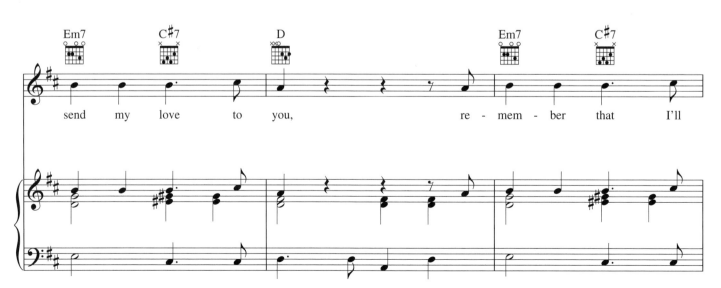

send my love to you, re - mem - ber that I'll

She Loves You

Words and Music by John Lennon and Paul McCartney

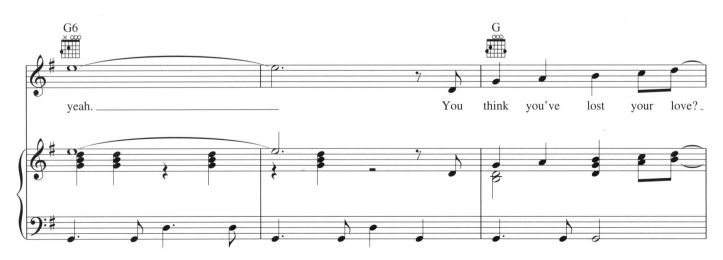

She's Leaving Home

Words and Music by John Lennon and Paul McCartney

step - ping out - side, she is free.
How could she do this to me?
meet - ing a man from the mo - tor trade.

She _____ is
She _____ is
She _____ is

We gave her most of our ___ lives.
We nev - er thought of our - selves.
What did we do that was ___ wrong?

leav - ing _____
leav - ing _____
hav - ing _____

Sac - ri - ficed most of our ___ lives. ___
Nev - er a thought for our - selves. ___
We did - n't know it was ___ wrong. ___

Strawberry Fields Forever

Words and Music by John Lennon and Paul McCartney

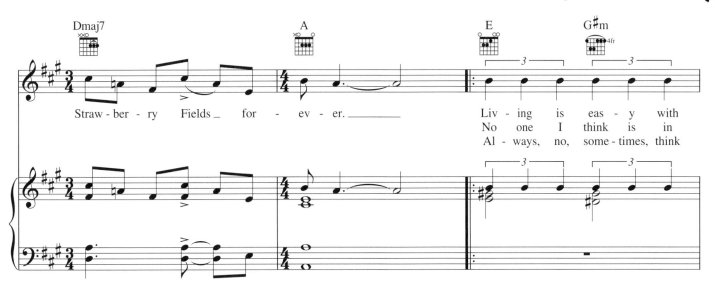

Straw - ber - ry Fields _ for - ev - er. _____ Liv - ing is eas - y with
No one I think is in
Al - ways, no, some - times, think

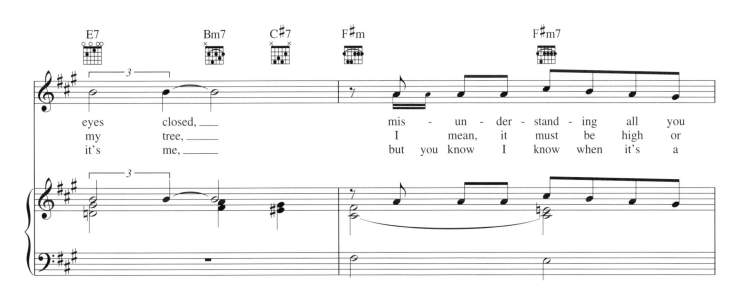

eyes closed, _____ mis - un - der - stand - ing all you
my tree, _____ I mean, it must be high or
it's me, _____ but you know I know when it's a

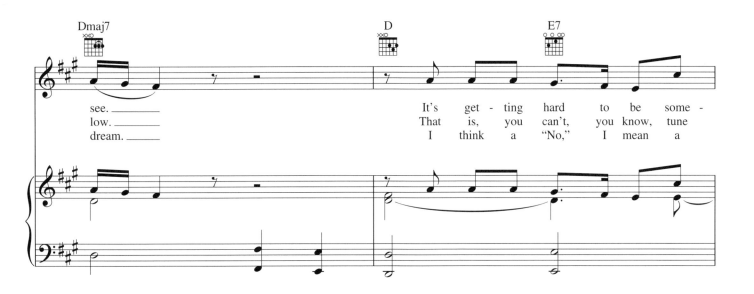

see. _____ It's get - ting hard to be some -
low. _____ That is, you can't, you know, tune
dream. _____ I think a "No," I mean a

one, but it all ___ works ___ out; it does - n't mat - ter much to
in, but it's all _____ right. That is, I think it's not too
"Yes," but it's all _____ wrong. That is, I think I dis - a -

me.
bad. }
gree.

Let me take you down, ___ 'cause I'm go - ing to ___

___ Straw - ber - ry Fields. Noth - ing is real, and

Ticket to Ride

Words and Music by John Lennon and Paul McCartney

We Can Work It Out

Words and Music by John Lennon and Paul McCartney

Yesterday

Words and Music by John Lennon and Paul McCartney

Moderately, with expression

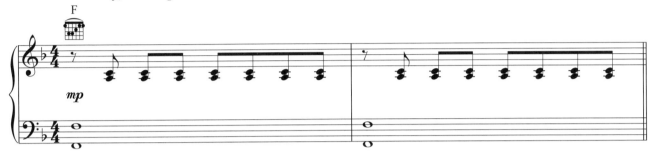

Yes - ter - day, _____ all my trou - bles seemed so
Sud - den - ly, _____ I'm not half the man I

far a - way, _____ now it looks as though _____ they're
used to be, _____ there's a shad - ow hang - ing

When I'm Sixty-Four

Words and Music by John Lennon and Paul McCartney

When I get old - er, los - ing my hair __ man - y years from now, __

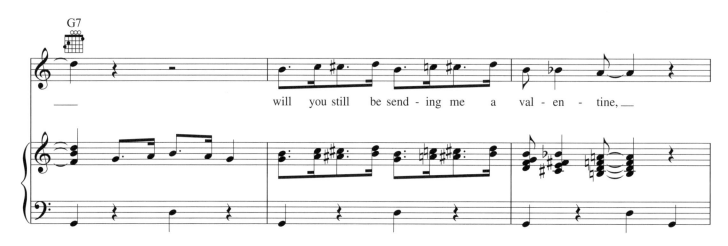

__ will you still be send - ing me a val - en - tine, __

With a Little Help from My Friends

Words and Music by John Lennon and Paul McCartney

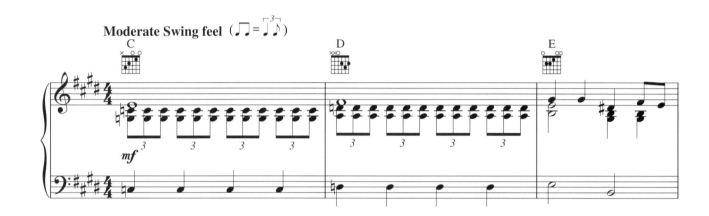

What would you think __ if I sang __ out of tune, would you stand
What do I do __ when my love __ is a-way? (Does it wor-
(Would you be-lieve __ in a love __ at first sight?) Yes, I'm cer-

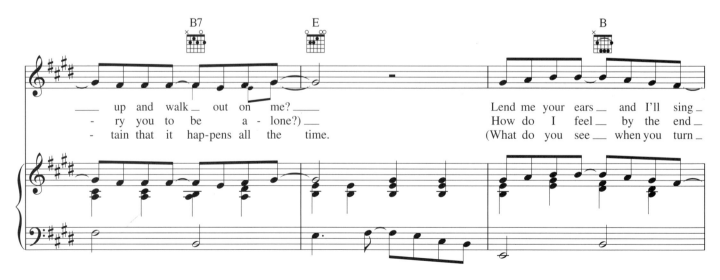

__ up and walk __ out on me? __
-ry you to be a-lone?) __
-tain that it hap-pens all the time.

Lend me your ears __ and I'll sing
How do I feel __ by the end
(What do you see __ when you turn __

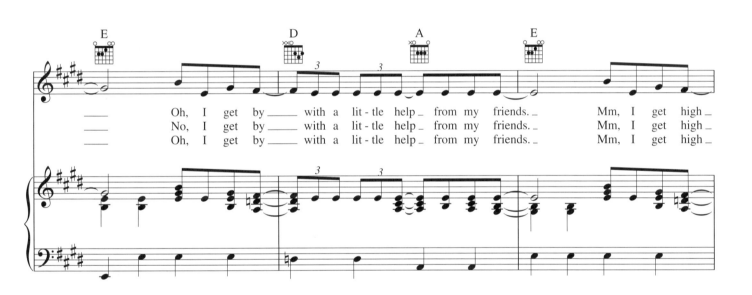

You've Got to Hide Your Love Away

Words and Music by John Lennon and Paul McCartney

Moderately, in 2

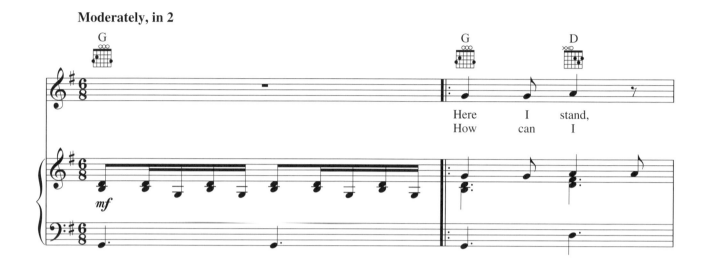

Here I stand,
How can I

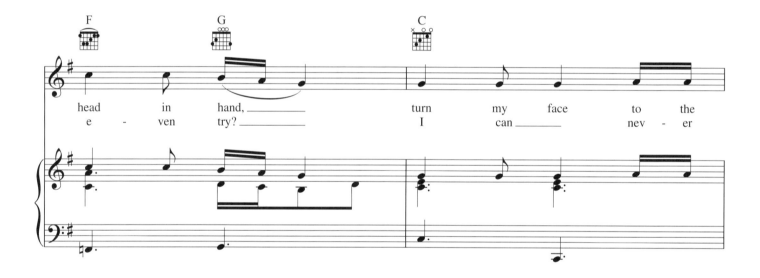

head in hand, _____ turn my face to the
e - ven try? _____ I can _____ nev - er

wall.   If she's gone, I can't go on, _____
win.   Hear - ing them, see - ing them, _____

You Won't See Me

Words and Music by John Lennon and Paul McCartney

LEARN YOUR FAVORITE SONGS
THE DUMMIES WAY®

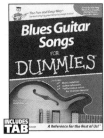

Big Books of Music

Our "Big Books" feature big selections of popular titles under one cover, perfect for performing musicians, music aficionados or the serious hobbyist. All books are arranged for piano, voice, and guitar, and feature stay-open binding, so the books lie flat without breaking the spine.

BIG BOOK OF BALLADS
62 songs.
00310485 ....$19.95

BIG BOOK OF BIG BAND HITS
84 songs.
00310701 ....$19.95

BIG BOOK OF BLUEGRASS SONGS
70 songs.
00311484 ....$19.95

BIG BOOK OF BLUES
80 songs.
00311843 ....$19.99

BIG BOOK OF BROADWAY
70 songs.
00311658 ....$19.95

BIG BOOK OF CHILDREN'S SONGS
55 songs.
00359261 ....$14.95

GREAT BIG BOOK OF CHILDREN'S SONGS
76 songs.
00310002 ....$14.95

FANTASTIC BIG BOOK OF CHILDREN'S SONGS
66 songs.
00311062 ....$17.95

MIGHTY BIG BOOK OF CHILDREN'S SONGS
65 songs.
00310467 ....$14.95

REALLY BIG BOOK OF CHILDREN'S SONGS
63 songs.
00310372 ....$16.95

BIG BOOK OF CHILDREN'S MOVIE SONGS
66 songs.
00310731 ....$19.95

BIG BOOK OF CHRISTMAS SONGS ·
126 songs.
00311520 ....$19.95

BIG BOOK OF CLASSIC ROCK
77 songs.
00310801 ....$22.95

BIG BOOK OF CLASSICAL MUSIC
100 songs.
00310508 ....$19.95

BIG BOOK OF CONTEMPORARY CHRISTIAN FAVORITES
50 songs.
00310021 ....$19.95

BIG BOOK OF COUNTRY MUSIC
63 songs.
00310188 ....$19.95

BIG BOOK OF COUNTRY ROCK
64 songs.
00311748 ....$19.99

BIG BOOK OF DISCO & FUNK
70 songs.
00310878 ....$19.95

BIG BOOK OF EARLY ROCK N' ROLL
99 songs.
00310398 ....$19.95

BIG BOOK OF '50S & '60S SWINGING SONGS
67 songs.
00310982 ....$19.95

BIG BOOK OF FOLK POP ROCK
79 songs.
00311125 ....$24.95

BIG BOOK OF FRENCH SONGS
70 songs.
00311154 ....$19.95

BIG BOOK OF GERMAN SONGS
78 songs.
00311816 ....$19.99

BIG BOOK OF GOSPEL SONGS
100 songs.
00310604 ....$19.95

BIG BOOK OF HYMNS
125 hymns.
00310510 ....$17.95

BIG BOOK OF IRISH SONGS
76 songs.
00310981 ....$19.95

BIG BOOK OF ITALIAN FAVORITES
80 songs.
00311185 ....$19.95

BIG BOOK OF JAZZ
75 songs.
00311557 ....$19.95

BIG BOOK OF LATIN AMERICAN SONGS
89 songs.
00311562 ....$19.95

BIG BOOK OF LOVE SONGS
80 songs.
00310784 ....$19.95

BIG BOOK OF MOTOWN
84 songs.
00311061 ....$19.95

BIG BOOK OF MOVIE MUSIC
72 songs.
00311582 ....$19.95

BIG BOOK OF NOSTALGIA
158 songs.
00310004 ....$19.95

BIG BOOK OF OLDIES
73 songs.
00310756 ....$19.95

BIG BOOK OF RAGTIME PIANO
63 songs.
00311749 ....$19.95

BIG BOOK OF RHYTHM & BLUES
67 songs.
00310169 ....$19.95

BIG BOOK OF ROCK
78 songs.
00311566 ....$22.95

BIG BOOK OF ROCK BALLADS
67 songs.
00311839 ....$22.99

BIG BOOK OF SOUL
71 songs.
00310771 ....$19.95

BIG BOOK OF STANDARDS
86 songs.
00311667 ....$19.95

BIG BOOK OF SWING
84 songs.
00310359 ....$19.95

BIG BOOK OF TORCH SONGS
75 songs.
00310561 ....$19.95

BIG BOOK OF TV THEME SONGS
78 songs.
00310504 ....$19.99

BIG BOOK OF WEDDING MUSIC
77 songs.
00311567 ....$19.95